HEAL'S

is delighted to support

D0100968

International
Arts and Crafts

Sir Ambrose Heal, born 1872, fourth-generation descendant of the founder of the home furnishing firm, was both an inspired shopkeeper and brilliant furniture designer. He embraced the Arts and Crafts movement, recognising how it could be used to improve everyday design and playing a key role in bringing it to a much wider audience.

We hope that visitors to the exhibition will be inspired by both the creativity of the movement and by its exacting standards of good design, quality materials and fine workmanship, values that are just as relevant at Heal's today.

Andrea Warden
CEO Heal's

The Arts and Crafts Movement

The Arts and Crafts Movement was one of the most influential, profound and far-reaching design movements of modern times. It began in Britain around 1880 and quickly spread across America and Europe before emerging finally as the Mingei (Folk Crafts) movement in Japan.

It was a movement born of ideals. It grew out of a concern for the effects of industrialisation: on design, on traditional skills and on the lives of ordinary people. In response, it established a new set of principles for living and working. It advocated the reform of art at every level and across a broad social spectrum, and it turned the home into a work of art.

The movement took its name from the Arts and Crafts Exhibition Society, founded in 1887, but it encompassed a very wide range of like-minded societies, workshops and manufacturers. Other countries adapted Arts and Crafts philosophies according to their own needs. While the work may be visually very different, it is united by the ideals that lie behind it.

Type of Membership

○ Standard £50   ○ Concessions £45

○ Student £20 (Graduation date) _ _ / _ _

○ Contributing £250

Method of Payment

○ Cash   ○ Cheque (payable to Friends of the V&A)

○ Credit Card

   ○ Amex   ○ Visa   ○ Mastercard   ○ Artscard   ○ Switch

   Card No. _ _ _ _ _ _ _ _ _ _ _ _ _ _ _ _ (_ _ _ _)

   Valid from date _ _ / _ _   Expiry date _ _ / _ _   Issue No. _ _

Under Gift Aid legislation the Friends of the V&A can recover basic rate tax on your donation providing you pay income tax or capital gains tax in the tax year the donation is made is equal to the amount of relief the Friends of the V&A is claiming. The tax reclaimed would be 28.2% of your donation. If you are willing to participate in the Gift Aid scheme, please sign the Gift Aid declaration below. I hereby declare that I want all voluntary donations made to the Friends of the V&A to be treated as Gift Aid. I have read the note above and agree to notify you of any change in my circumstances.

○ I do not wish to Gift Aid my donation

Signature

Optional extra donation £   Total £

The data given on this form will be used for administrative, fundraising and marketing purposes only. It may be passed to third parties but will not be transferred to areas without adequate levels of privacy protection. For the purpose of the Data Protection Act 1998, the data controller is the Executive Committee. If you would prefer not to receive such mailings please tick here ○

V&A Membership is run by The Friends of the V&A, charity number 272056

V&A and You?

V&A members enjoy a range of benefits. These include unlimited free entry to all major exhibitions (with a guest), previews of new galleries and exhibitions, access to the new Members room, the V&A magazine, exclusive events, and special discounts and offers.

All levels of membership are also available as gifts. For further information visit the Information Desk or call 020 7942 2271.
www.vam.ac.uk

To become a member of the V&A simply fill
in the form below and you will automatically be entered for the prize draw. See separate card or ask at the Information desk for details.

Please hand the completed form in at the membership desk or post to V&A Membership, Cromwell Road, London, SW7 2RL

Application for Membership V&A No. (Office use only)

Title	Forename
Surname	Date of birth
Address	
	Postcode
Telephone	
Email	

Audioguide

The audio guide is provided by Antenna Audio
Standard rental price £3.50
Concessions and members £3.00

Events

An extensive programme of events and activities has been
arranged to complement the exhibition. It is suitable for
visitors with both general and specific interests and will
appeal to all ages. The programme focuses on craftsmanship
and the ideas behind Arts and Crafts designs, both in Britain
and abroad. It includes workshops, demonstrations, gallery
talks and lectures, as well as events for schools, families and
young people. Most are free and drop-in. For full details pick
up an exhibition leaflet at the Information Desk or visit
www.vam.ac.uk/artsandcrafts

Conference

International Arts and Crafts
Friday 22 & Saturday 23 April
For further details visit www.vam.ac.uk/artsandcrafts

Arts and Crafts and the permanent collection

You can see Arts and Crafts elsewhere in the V&A. Visit the
British Galleries, the Silver and 20th Century galleries, and the
Morris, Gamble and Poynter rooms, the V&A's first
refreshment rooms.

Illustrations (all details)

Artist-Craftsmen of the Mingei Movement

The Mingei movement was a modern craft movement. It championed the work of named artist-craftsmen who, by example, helped to preserve and raise the standards of traditional artisanal craft production threatened by industrialisation.

Four of the founding members of the Mingei movement were potters: the Englishman Bernard Leach, who lived in Japan from 1909 to 1920, Hamada Shōji, Kawai Kanjirō and Tomimoto Kenkichi. After the official launching of the Mingei movement in 1926, they were joined by the textile artist Serizawa Keisuke, the woodwork and lacquer artist Kuroda Tatsuaki, and the painter and woodblock-print artist Munakata Shikō.

The works created by these seven artist-craftsmen are concrete expressions of the enthusiasms and preoccupations of the artistic and intellectual circles in which they moved. They are undisputed classics from a seminal period in the development of Japanese crafts.

The Mikunisō

One of the most significant achievements of the Mingei movement was the establishment of a revolutionary new style of middle-class living. This combined old and new, east and west, rural and urban in a compelling hybrid that sought to meet the new economic and social conditions of early 20th-century Japan.

The first and most important Mingei building designed by Yanagi Sōetsu and his companions was the Mikunisō (Mikuni Villa). Initially this was built as a Folk Craft Pavilion for an exhibition in Tokyo in 1928. After the exhibition closed, a wealthy businessman bought the pavilion and converted it into a guest house in the grounds of his residence in the Mikuni district of Osaka.

The reconstruction displayed here is based on photographs and a bird's-eye view from the mid-1930s. It shows the interconnecting western-style dining room and Japanese-style reception room.

Historical Folk Crafts

The Mingei movement devoted a great deal of energy to collecting historical folk crafts. Central to this was the application of the principle of 'direct perception', the intuitive ability to discover beauty that was 'born' rather than 'made'. This reflected a belief on the part of Yanagi Sōetsu and his followers that true beauty could only be found in works created in a spirit of selfless innocence and in close harmony with nature.

The objects displayed here show the extensive range of folk crafts collected by Yanagi and other members of the Mingei movement. They feature works from all over Japan, including Okinawa in the south and Hokkaidō, home of the Ainu people, in the north. Also included are works from Korea and examples of vernacular furniture and ceramics from Britain. Four of the objects belong to the Japan Folk Crafts Museum in Tokyo. This was founded by Yanagi in 1936 and became the hub of a nationwide network of institutions that is still active today.

Japan 1926–1945

The Mingei (Folk Crafts) movement in Japan was led by the philosopher and critic Yanagi Sōetsu and officially established in 1926. It was equivalent to, and very largely inspired by, the Arts and Crafts Movement in Britain and Europe. John Ruskin and William Morris, whose work had been available since the 1880s, were major influences. Knowledge about subsequent developments in Europe also reached Japan.

As with other Arts and Crafts developments, the Mingei movement emerged during a time of rapid change. In Japan, this involved westernisation as well as industrialisation and urban growth. Mingei philosophy recognised this international and urban dimension, but at the same time asserted a new sense of Japanese national identity.

Introducing the idea that humble goods could be inherently beautiful, leaders of the Mingei movement advocated the use of historical folk crafts as the starting point for new craft production. They assembled extensive collections and founded museums to house them. They also created model rooms in an ambitious attempt to persuade the middle classes to adopt a new hybrid lifestyle that combined both Japanese and western features.

Germany

It was in Germany that the relationship between art, craft and industry was perhaps most successfully worked out. Companies, workshops and art schools explored the design and manufacture of good quality, everyday goods as a means of boosting local economies, as well as achieving social reform and lifting the status of the decorative arts.

Artist's colonies such as the one at Darmstadt were founded on the model of British groups such as the Guild of Handicraft. They too shared common views on materials and craftsmanship and aimed to elevate the status of the decorative arts.

However, the British model was thought to be too anti-industrial in spirit. In Germany it was legitimate to use technology as a means of achieving efficient production, so long as quality was maintained in the end product. In retrospect, the German interpretation of Arts and Crafts proved to be one of the most long-lasting and influential.

Scandinavia and Central Europe

Unlike Britain, large parts of Europe remained rural economies with little industrial development. Consequently, the key concerns that shaped the Arts and Crafts Movement in Hungary, Russia and Scandinavia were very different.

In the Scandinavian countries greater political independence created a sense of nationalism and a need for a new cultural identity. In Central Europe, severe social deprivation co-existed with a desire to preserve the many local cultures. This led to the rediscovery of peasant and vernacular architecture, as well as folk art, music and literature.

Designers, even in physically remote countries like Finland and Norway, were able to follow developments in Britain and mainstream Europe. The Arts and Crafts models of tradition and innovation provided a framework in which individuals or small workshops could create new and distinctive work. This revival and survival of traditional handicrafts, however, still relied on the patronage of the upper-middle classes.

Vienna

As capital of the Austro-Hungarian Empire, Vienna held an elite position. It was a great cultural and intellectual centre, at the forefront of developments in music, psychology, the natural sciences and the visual arts.

The role of patron, more often associated with the aristocracy, was assumed by the wealthy upper-middle class. New design reflected the sophisticated, avant-garde mood of both designers and patrons, but also benefited from the Viennese tradition of fine craftsmanship.

In 1897 progressive artists in the city turned their backs on the art establishment and joined together to form 'Secession' exhibition groups. They connected with the latest artistic developments abroad and invited artists from France, Belgium, England and Scotland to take part in the eighth Vienna Secession in 1900. The unity of arts and crafts was a constant theme and in 1903 Josef Hoffmann, Koloman Moser and Otto Wagner founded the Wiener Werkstätte for the production of well designed objects for the home.

Europe 1890–1914

Across Europe, the Arts and Crafts Movement saw a revival of traditional techniques and materials and the creation of new forms that were both ageless and innovative.

Arts and Crafts ideals developed in a number of regions, including Russia, Scandinavia, Germany and the Austro-Hungarian Empire. In a period of political and social turmoil, the decorative arts were an area in which ideas of national identity, social organisation and life in an industrial society could be explored.

However, the level to which Arts and Crafts practices, in particular attitudes to industrial manufacture, were fully accepted or merely adapted was very varied. In the less industrialised regions of Europe nationalism was a more compelling factor.

As in Britain and America, the homes designed and built by artists and architects for their own use were proof of the idea that the home, as well as life within it, could become a work of art. These houses drew on national and local traditions, celebrated individual expression and provided an ideal of domesticity.

Greene & Greene and the American North West

The natural beauty, inviting climate and unique local materials of California encouraged a very individual response to Arts and Crafts ideals. Its distant location meant that Arts and Crafts activity was quite isolated, which also made for a distinctive approach to design.

Charles and Henry Greene were California's foremost Arts and Crafts architects and the designers of extraordinarily fine bespoke craftsmanship. The Greenes saw the house as a total work of art and created furniture specifically for each room. Their richly coloured and beautifully crafted interiors are notable for the exquisite joinery in sumptuous Californian redwoods and for the subtle play of light through stained-glass windows and doors.

San Francisco was then recovering from the devastating 1906 earthquake. This provided many opportunities for new workshops and furnishing styles, most notably those of the Furniture Shop and the metalworker Dirk van Erp.

Frank Lloyd Wright and the Prairie School 1890–1910

Chicago was at the heart of American expansion and economic growth. It provided fertile ground for the development of the Arts and Crafts Movement and became the home of early Arts and Crafts societies and projects.

The city became the base for the architects and designers of the Prairie School, one of the most innovative manifestations of the Arts and Crafts Movement in America. The flat prairie landscape of the Midwest inspired Frank Lloyd Wright and his contemporaries to develop a radical, earth-hugging domestic architecture as a contrast to the new city skyscrapers.

Progressive architects and designers such as Frank Lloyd Wright introduced revolutionary changes in domestic design. Designing across all media, they treated both inside and out as a complete work of art. They opened up interiors, banished applied ornament and instead integrated features such as stained glass into spaces defined by the furniture. They also sought to bring nature into their design by using native plants as abstract motifs.

A Craftsman Room

Gustav Stickley's magazine, *The Craftsman*, was one of the most far-reaching publications of the Arts and Crafts Movement in America. From 1904 it featured a series of 'Craftsman' homes designed and built by Stickley's Craftsman Workshops. They included models for a range of incomes, from the smallest cottages upwards. Although he thought the country was the best place to live, Stickley's designs could be adapted for suburban use.

Craftsman homes illustrated the ideals of 'honesty, simplicity and usefulness'. Stickley believed that the living room was the heart of the home, a place to nurture family life and a sanctuary for the working man. Its furniture should be simple and harmonise with the woodwork in colour and finish.

This recreation of a Craftsman living room is largely based on a design published in *The Craftsman* in March 1904. The post-and-panel detail is taken from a living room published in 1907.

Gustav Stickley and the East Coast

Arts and Crafts societies and experimental communities, modelled on British prototypes, were established in and around Massachusetts and New York in the early 1890s. Among the most notable initiatives were the Roycroft Shops and the Byrdcliffe Colony, both in New York state, and Gustav Stickley's Craftsman Farms in New Jersey.

Perhaps more than anyone else, Stickley defined the Arts and Crafts Movement as it evolved in America. Although he fully subscribed to Arts and Crafts ideals, his approach was more commercially aware. Stickley sought economic viability as well as moral satisfaction.

He operated as an entrepreneur, designer and furniture manufacturer. In 1898 he founded the Craftsman Workshops in Syracuse, New York, for the production of furniture, metalwork and textiles. From 1901 to 1916 he published *The Craftsman*, an influential magazine in which he illustrated his own work as well as that from Britain, mainland Europe and other parts of America.

America 1890–1916

America embraced the Arts and Crafts Movement and made it its own. The movement flourished on the East Coast, in the Midwest and in California, and included major figures such as Frank Lloyd Wright, Charles and Henry Greene, and Gustav Stickley. Despite its European origins, the movement acquired a particularly American form and expression that reflected the confidence of the relatively young nation. This can be seen especially in a radical new approach to the house and its interior, which remains influential to this day.

Exchanges of ideas between Britain and America were frequent and visible. The work of Ruskin, Morris, Ashbee and Baillie Scott was well known and had a significant influence. But American Arts and Crafts designers also looked to their native landscape and climate, to their own heritage and even to Japan. They took a much more commercial approach to Arts and Crafts, but maintained a strong sense of individuality and national identity in their work.

Sidney Barnsley's Cottage

Sidney Barnsley was an architect, but in 1893 he moved from London to the Cotswolds to make furniture using traditional methods. He lived in a cottage converted from the farm outbuildings in the grounds of Pinbury Park, an Elizabethan house that had been leased by his brother. Nearby lived Ernest Gimson, who had also moved with them from London to establish his own workshop.

The simplicity of the cottage furnishings, with its stone floor and plastered walls, evoked a hard-working outdoor country life. Together, Gimson and the Barnsleys got to know local craftsmen and learnt their ways. At home, they kept chickens, brewed cider and made their own bread.

The furnishings in Sidney Barnsley's cottage included this large oak dresser which he made himself. There was also a traditional inglenook, with built-in furniture around the fireplace. This arrangement featured in many Arts and Crafts houses, making the hearth the focus of the home, its warm heart.

Arts and Crafts in the Countryside

According to C.R. Ashbee, one of the leading figures of the movement, 'the proper place for the Arts and Crafts is in the country'. For many artists, living and working in the countryside was the ideal to which they aspired. At the heart of the Arts and Crafts Movement lay a belief in the closeness of mankind to nature and a nostalgia for rural life and local traditions—concepts that appear throughout the literature, music and art of the period.

Followers of the movement established workshops across Britain, in places like the Cotswolds, the Lake District, Surrey and Cornwall. All these locations offered picturesque landscapes, existing craft skills and, importantly, rail links for access to patrons and the London market.

Arts and Crafts makers revived rural craft traditions and offered employment to local people. The movement endured far longer in the countryside than in the city and its impact on rural areas was significant and far-reaching.

A London Home

The urban home of William Ward-Higgs, a successful solicitor in the City of London, and his wife Haydee reflected their advanced artistic tastes. In 1896 they commissioned the architect C. F. A. Voysey to help furnish the house that they had leased in the London suburb of Bayswater.

Voysey often took a purist approach to his interiors, carefully designing every detail, but the rooms in this house were eclectically furnished. It was a typical Arts and Crafts urban home, sophisticated and intellectual, but also comfortable and practical.

The furnishings combined the new and old. Voysey designed several items, including a desk and armchair for Haydee Ward-Higgs. They were mainly simple, architectural pieces, made of plain oak with minimal decoration.

Apart from designing to commission, Voysey sold many of his designs to manufacturers. He worked with a wide range of materials, including furniture, wallpaper, carpets and textiles, metalwork and ceramics.

Arts and Crafts in the City

The Arts and Crafts Movement flourished in large cities such as London, Birmingham, Manchester, Glasgow and Edinburgh. These urban centres had the infrastructure of organisations and patronage that allowed the movement to gather pace. The work itself was created in a variety of situations, ranging from individual and small workshops to larger manufacturers.

Exhibition societies, initially in London and subsequently throughout Britain, gave the movement its name, public identity and a forum for discussion. Progressive new art schools, such as the Central School of Arts and Crafts in London, emphasised handwork and craftsmanship. They encouraged the development of workshops and individuals, as well as the revival of techniques like enamelling, embroidery and calligraphy.

Designers and manufacturers forged new relationships and were able to sell their Arts and Crafts goods through shops such as Morris & Co., Heal's and Liberty's. All this helped the movement reach a much wider audience. Its patrons were mainly fashionable and artistically aware individuals, but they also included institutions such as the Church.

Britain 1880–1914

In Britain, the Arts and Crafts Movement flourished from about 1880. At its heart lay a concern for the role of the craftsman. Inspired by the ideas of John Ruskin and William Morris, it advocated a revival of traditional handicrafts, a return to a simpler way of life and an improvement in the design of ordinary domestic objects.

The Arts and Crafts Exhibition Society, which gave the movement its name, and other organisations such as the Art Workers Guild, worked to raise the status of the decorative arts and of the individual craftsman. They were also determined to interact with the commercial world and influence industrial design.

There was both a sophisticated urban dimension and a radical rural expression to the Arts and Crafts Movement. It evolved and flourished in the city, but the strong pull of the countryside and the simple life that it promised led many to leave the city and establish new ways of living and working. The British Arts and Crafts model of workshop practice and individual creativity was to have a worldwide impact.

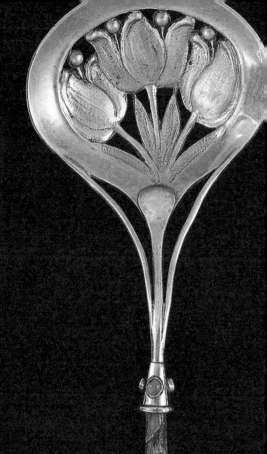

This was a movement unlike any that had gone before. Its pioneering spirit of reform, and the value it placed on the quality of materials and design, as well as life, shaped the world we live in today.

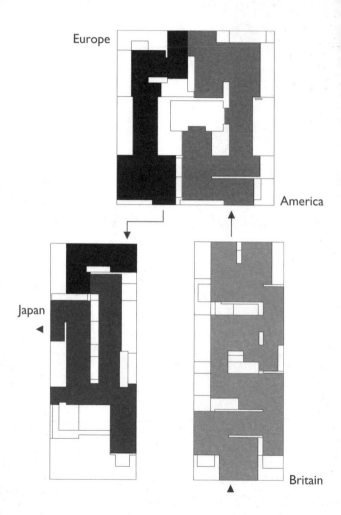

Origins of the Movement

In Britain the disastrous effects of industrial manufacture and unregulated trade had been recognised since about 1840. But it was not until the 1860s and 1870s that architects, designers and artists began to pioneer new approaches to design and the decorative arts. These, in turn, led to the foundation of the Arts and Crafts Movement.

The two most influential figures were the theorist and critic John Ruskin and the designer, writer and activist William Morris. Ruskin examined the relationship between art, society and labour. Morris put Ruskin's philosophies into practice, placing great value on work, the joy of craftsmanship and the natural beauty of materials.

By the 1880s Morris had become an internationally renowned and commercially successful designer and manufacturer. New guilds and societies began to take up his ideas, presenting for the first time a unified approach among architects, painters, sculptors and designers. In doing so, they brought Arts and Crafts ideals to a wider public.